FORGIVE US OUR
DEBTS

WHEN IS IT OKAY FOR CHRISTIANS
TO FILE BANKRUPTCY?

ANNE-MARIE L. BOWEN, ESQ.

Liability Disclaimer

What People are Saying...

"I don't know a Baptist Pastor who could have researched and written a better book than this. There are 47,000 Southern Baptist churches in the United States, and every one of them should have a copy of this book."

Tim Grosshans, Senior Pastor
First Baptist Church of Winter Garden

"This well written and easy to read book will be a blessing to those hungering to learn what the Bible says about debt and forgiveness. Anne-Marie Bowen offers hope in a conflicted world coupled with practical advice on living simply and seeking peace."

Pastor, Catholic Church

"This is a wonderful, practical book which is also full of grace and hope. Those who read it will be blessed with the gift of encouragement and reassurance."

Rev. Melanie Ruta
Presbyterian Church (USA)

"I couldn't stop reading this book. Anne-Marie Bowen does a great job of making the theological practical. She reminds Christians everywhere that God still loves them, no matter what their circumstances. This book will be a blessing to many who need to hear this timely message."

Rev. Edward DeWitt
Pastor, Redeemer Lutheran Church

"Anne-Marie L. Bowen's new book Forgive Us Our Debts: When is it Okay for Christians to File Bankruptcy fills a tremendous need for people of faith. Anne-Marie shares biblical and U.S. history of the necessity for laws forgiving debt, as well as an overview of bankruptcy law today. Her book turns filing bankruptcy into a spiritual healing experience. I intend to have copies of this book on hand at all times in my office to share with my bankruptcy clients. Thank you, Anne-Marie, for undertaking this project that God laid on your heart—to heal the sick and tired, raise the depressed in spirit, and to cast out the demons of guilt and unforgiveness. You are a true disciple of Jesus."

Kathryn A. Hathaway, Bankruptcy Attorney and Author of Amazon Best Seller, Rise Like a Phoenix: The 12 Steps of Bankruptcy

Contact Information

For comments to the author, scheduling interviews, or speaking engagements, contact that author at:

Anne-Marie L. Bowen, Esq.
Anne-Marie L. Bowen, P.A.
816 North Thornton Avenue
Orlando, FL 32803

407-228-1300

www.bowenbankruptcylaw.com

Give this book to someone who would find it helpful. Additional copies may be ordered from Anne-Marie L. Bowen at 407-228-1300 or www.bowenbankruptcylaw.com or through the publisher at www.afreshpublishing.com, or at www.amazon.com.

Dedication

To my Mom, Marie R. Lindsey,
(November 5, 1930-November 20, 2017),
a woman of faith who showed me daily,
in word and deed, what it is to be a Christian.

Table of Contents

Introduction

FOR AT LEAST TEN YEARS I have contemplated writing a book about Christians and bankruptcy. Over the many years I have practiced law, I've seen how Christians more than others are so guilt-ridden and torn when they need to file bankruptcy. They feel as if they are sinning against God when they can't pay back a debt they incurred. They often tell me, "I wasn't raised like this," or "My father would kill me if he knew I was even thinking about bankruptcy." I have wanted to give comfort to those clients in a very tangible way, and I thought a book would be a great way to do that.

As time has gone on, many obstacles have been placed in my way. Chief among them, my own doubts. What can I say as a person who has read the entire Bible several times but who can't readily quote the Bible off the top of my head like so many Christians can? What can I say? How can I help? Who will listen?

I've given this a great deal of thought. *I feel called, but not qualified.* I've never gone to Seminary. I'm not a Bible Scholar. I didn't study Theology. I don't have degrees in anything but Business and Law. I have the wrong kind of Doctorate Degree, so how can I possibly write a book about Christians and bankruptcy? But Samuel was called in 1 Samuel Chapter 3. He didn't recognize it at first, but then said, "Here I am." So, here I am, too.

Well, I know a good bit about bankruptcy having worked in the field for many years. And I know some about the Bible, so I have undertaken to study the Bible to see what God's Word has to say about all this. So, while I can quote some Scriptures now, I rely on the Holy Spirit to guide me in interpretations. As discussed, I'm no Biblical expert. But, God gave me a brain and has laid this project on my heart, so "I can do all things through Him who strengthens me." (Philippians 4:13 (ESV)).

I hope I haven't dissuaded you from reading further. Hopefully, you'll gain some knowledge and understanding which will help you find peace in your present circumstances. C.S. Lewis wrote in one of his books years ago that if you find anything of value, use it, and if you find anything bad, forget it. I'm paraphrasing, but I think Lewis got this thought from 1 Thessalonians 5:21 (NLT): "Test everything that is said. Hold on to what is good."

And so, dear readers, if this book can help you to understand what God has to say about bankruptcy and debt, and when it is okay for Christians to file bankruptcy, then please use it and let it minister to you. If I get something wrong from your understanding, feel free to discuss it with your own Pastor or a trusted friend.

In my Church ministry, I love Isaiah 50:4 which reads,

The Sovereign Lord has given me
a well-instructed tongue,
to know the word
that sustains the weary.

I believe this passage applies to this written book as well as to my oral speaking. I pray that I may say something to help the weary soul find peace, or perhaps rouse those who need it to take action.

Blessings,

Anne-Marie L. Bowen

Follower of Jesus

· CHAPTER 1 ·

Forgive Us Our Debts

ON THE DAY I WROTE THE INTRODUCTION to this book, I had a couple come in to see me for an initial consultation. Bob[1] and Joy had experienced all forms of the most common reasons people need to file bankruptcy, namely: health problems, job loss, divorce, and business failure. Bob was in an accident years ago, which later caused seizures. He was diagnosed with epilepsy and other cognitive problems. He had an excellent job with a high security clearance working for the government for more than twenty-five years. However, his health was failing him even though he was only about 50 years old. His first wife left, and he had ended up with a lot of bills related to the divorce. He kept working as best he could, but eventually

---

[1] The names and identifying details in this book have been changed to protect client confidentiality and to protect the privacy of individuals.

he was forced to take a medical retirement long before he wanted to.

Bob and his second wife Joy decided to invest all his 401(k) Retirement Savings into a faith-based business. They thought that if Bob couldn't work in his professional field, he could work in a store. So, they partnered with another "Christian" couple. Unfortunately, their business partners weren't very Christian after all. They stole from them, defrauded them, and embezzled money. Bob and Joy were left with nothing in very short order.

They talked to a lawyer who found out the IRS had a massive lien against the ex-partners, and although Bob and Joy might help the authorities put the ex-partners in jail, they would never collect any money from them, and the stress of it all would only hurt Bob's health. So, with the help of their Pastor, they decided to forgive their ex-partners and move on with their lives as best they could.

At this point, they've lost all their life savings, career, jobs, business; but, they haven't lost their faith, thank God. Still, they struggle with the decision to file bankruptcy because they were raised to always pay their bills. I said, "You know, you've forgiven the people that defrauded you. They stole merchandize from you, they ran up your credit cards, they took your money. And yet, you forgave them. So, why shouldn't you be forgiven too?" I was able to quote them Matthew 6:12 which says,

Forgive us our debts, as we also have forgiven our debtors.

This couple is living the Lord's Prayer, and they didn't even know it.

As an aside, I want to note the great irony here. I had just finished writing the Introduction to this book where I said how I can't always quote Scripture off the top of my head, and here I did it! God is so good. And this was a Scripture Bob and Joy really needed to hear at that exact moment.

There is a parable in the Bible found at Matthew 18: 23-27 about a king who was settling accounts with his servants. One servant owed the king a very large debt he could not repay. The master was going to sell off the servant and his family to pay the debt, but when the servant dropped to his knees and begged, the master took pity on him and cancelled the entire debt.

This story tells us that God forgives debt. This parable is specifically about forgiveness, and there is no question that through the character of the master, we can rest assured that God forgives us our debts.

But, there is more to this story…Matthew 18:28-35 goes on to talk about how this same servant who owed so much money, but whose debt was completely forgiven by his master, treated someone indebted to him. This servant had another servant who owed him but a very small sum. He

FORGIVE US OUR DEBTS

demanded payment. The fellow servant begged for mercy, just as the first servant begged his master, but rather than forgiving the small debt after he had been forgiven a large debt, he had the poor man thrown in jail (i.e. Debtor's Prison), until the debt could be paid off. When word of this treachery got back to the master, he handed over the ungrateful, unmerciful servant to be tortured. The lesson here is that when you are forgiven, you must also forgive others who owe you. *"Forgive us our debts as we also have forgiven our debtors." (Matthew 6:12).*

Let's talk some more about forgiveness and sins. I have heard people say many times that they feel so badly about considering bankruptcy because they think it is sinful to not repay their debt. They feel like they made a promise to pay their bills and they will break their promise by not paying these obligations. However, they also promised to support their spouse and children. When you can't put food on the table or keep the lights on, or keep the roof over your heads, because you don't have enough money left after paying your credit card bills and loans, this is a problem. It seems to me that it is not a sin to put your family's needs before your creditors' demands.

So, I personally do not consider bankruptcy to be a sin. I don't think I could sleep at night if I thought I was helping people sin every day. We know that sin separates us from God. We feel guilt at small things, so I would definitely feel guilt if I thought helping people file bankruptcy was a big sin.

But even if I am wrong, and you have sinned by not paying all your debt, then please remember that our God is loving, and kind, and merciful. God wipes out all our sins. Isaiah 43:25 reads, He "remembers your sins no more."

I have swept away your offenses
like a cloud,
Your sins like the morning mist.
Return to me,
For I have redeemed you.

Isaiah 44:22

And how about the Lord's Prayer as told by Luke:

Forgive us our sins,
for we also forgive everyone
who sins against us.

Luke 11:4

Finally, read these comforting words:

Be kind and compassionate
to one another,
forgiving each other,
just as in Christ
God forgave you.

Ephesians 4:32

God forgives us all our transgressions if we but ask with a sincere heart.

If we confess our sins,
He is faithful and just
and will forgive us our sins
and purify us
from all unrighteousness.

1 John 1:9

He asks us to forgive each other. I believe, that we need to forgive <u>ourselves</u>, too.

So many times we beat ourselves up over and over again. We may have confessed a sin to God, and truly repented, but then we seem to discount God's Grace by still feeling guilty about the same sin we've already confessed and already been forgiven. This constant guilt over the same thing is not healthy. Also, I had a Pastor who once told me that if you still feel like God couldn't forgive you, you are committing a new sin – that of pride! So, please, be kind to yourself, be compassionate to yourself as you are towards others, and most importantly, forgive yourself for getting into a financial mess.

Forgive as the Lord forgave you.

Colossians 3:13

Questions for Reflection

1. What problems have you encountered that caused you to get into financial trouble? (For example, health problems, job loss, loss of overtime, divorce, business failure, overspending, helping family too much, etc.)

_____

_____

_____

_____

_____

_____

2. Have you ever lent money to someone? If they didn't pay you back, how did you feel? Would you forgive them?

_____

_____

_____

_____

_____

_____

3. Do you believe owing money you can't pay back is a sin?
If so, why?

_____

_____

_____

_____

_____

_____

_____

4. Do you believe God forgives your sins if you ask Him
with a sincere heart of repentance?

_____

_____

_____

_____

_____

_____

_____

5. When have you forgiven someone who wronged you? How did you feel after you let their transgression go?

_____

_____

_____

_____

_____

_____

_____

6. "You are worthy of God's forgiveness and love." How does this make you feel?

_____

_____

_____

_____

_____

_____

_____

· C H A P T E R   2 ·

Cancellation of Debts and the Jubilee

IN ANCIENT TIMES, AS IT IS NOW, God knew that people would get into financial trouble. How do we know this? Because the Old Testament tells us. Deuteronomy 15 discusses the year of cancelling debts. "At the end of every seven years you must cancel debts." (Deuteronomy 15:1). "Every seventh year we...will cancel all debts." (Nehemiah 10:31). In addition, the slaves were to be set free in the seventh year. (Deuteronomy 15:12).

So many people today are slaves to their debt. They spend their days and nights juggling bills, like plates in the air, trying not to let anything drop, lest it break.

One client, Karen, told me that she dreaded checking her emails to see what new bills and threatening letters and messages came in. She had trouble sleeping at night because she just could not turn off her brain filled with fear and worry about how she was going to make it. After we discussed all her options, she chose to file a Chapter 7 bankruptcy case. She received a Discharge, which is a legal cancellation of dischargeable debts. She was released of her debt and couldn't have been more grateful. She felt God had mercy on her by giving her a second chance.

God tells us to rest on the Sabbath, or seventh day each week. He also prescribed a Sabbath year to be celebrated every seven years. In Leviticus 25 we learn about the Jubilee Year. Every 50 years the slaves were to be set free and the land was to be returned to its original owners. The 50-year period was arrived at by taking seven Sabbatical years, which occur every seven years, or seven times seven, which equals 49 years. So in the following, or 50th year, the Jubilee is celebrated. Freedom is restored for all.

For many, many years, the bankruptcy law in the United States provided that you could file Chapter 7 bankruptcy every seven years, just like the Sabbath years of the Old Testament. This is directly related to the cancellation of debts proclaimed in Deuteronomy. The bankruptcy law was changed in 2005 when, for the first time ever, the time between Chapter 7 bankruptcy cases was increased from seven to eight years. I guess the Biblical teaching of seven years was ignored or forgotten by Congress!

We learn of the Lord's favor in Isaiah 61:

The Spirit of the Sovereign Lord
is on me,
because the Lord has anointed me
to proclaim good news to the poor.

Your personal good news is that you may be forgiven of your debts through bankruptcy. Replace your shame with God's Grace. Celebrate your personal Jubilee, and let this be your year of favor from our Lord. (See Isaiah 61:2).

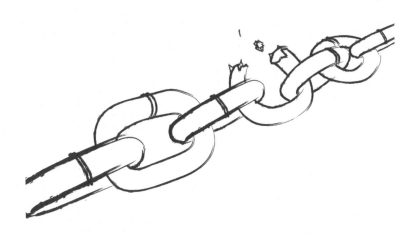

Questions for Reflection

1. Read Deuteronomy Chapter 15 about the year for cancelling debts. Why do you think God set a period of seven years to forgive debts?

_____

_____

_____

_____

_____

2. Do you feel like you are a slave to your debts? Are you losing sleep at night worrying about how you will pay all your bills? Are you tired of being so tired? Should you consider doing something about it?

_____

_____

_____

_____

3. Read Leviticus Chapter 25 about the Jubilee Year. Why do you think God built in an absolute year of freedom for all?

_____

_____

_____

_____

_____

_____

_____

4. Do you see the correlation between the Chapter 7 bankruptcy discharge being allowed every seven (now eight) years and the Sabbath years? Why do you think our founding fathers offered people a cancellation of debts?

_____

_____

_____

_____

_____

_____

5. Read Isaiah Chapter 61. Do you believe in the Lord's favor? Will you consider replacing your shame with God's grace? How do you feel knowing that it is possible to experience a personal Jubilee?

CHAPTER 3

Tithing

THE BIBLE DISCUSSES TITHING and giving of your first fruits in multiple places. For some people, however, this is not always possible.

I once had a client, Edward, who was an elderly gentleman. He was a life-long Baptist; however, he stopped going to Church after his wife of more than 60 years died. I didn't understand why he would stop attending services and getting the love, support, and comfort of his church family after his heart was broken. He explained to me that he could no longer attend church because the Bible says he must tithe. Now that he lost his wife's income after she died, he could no longer afford to give to the church because he was struggling to pay his lot rent on his mobile home and his electric, and other bills. He absolutely could not afford to tithe or give any money on his small Social Security check, which was his sole source of income.

This really bothered me that a man who spent his entire life living uprightly and staying so faithful to his Baptist Church felt he was no longer allowed to attend. I did not tell him to go find another denomination or church. Rather, I strongly suggested he go meet with his own Pastor. Tell him what is going on so that he understands your situation. After some more encouragement, Edward finally got up the nerve to meet with his Pastor. He called me immediately afterwards. Edward was elated that his Pastor welcomed him home to church with loving arms. His Pastor assured him that the whole church community was there for him, even though Edward could not financially contribute at this point in his life. What Edward could continue to do was pray for them – in this case it was the "widower's might," as opposed to the "widow's mite!" (See, Mark 12:41-44; Luke 21:1-4).

Second Corinthians 9:6-15 directs us to give what we have decided in our hearts to give, not reluctantly or under compulsion. You see, God doesn't need our money, but we need to give to bless others. "For the Lord loves a cheerful giver." (2 Corinthians 9:7). But it's hard to give cheerfully when you can't pay your bills.

My husband works at our church as the Director of Music, so we've been actively involved in church our whole lives. We understand the practicalities that your church needs money to pay its mortgage or rent, electric bill, salaries, insurance, etc., just like you and your family need money to live. So, those who are able, need to give to bless so that others are served and blessed. However, if you are giving with pain, it's just giving to give and not giving with the right heart to bless others. It's hard to serve God when you are busy serving your debt. "You cannot serve both God and money." (Matthew 6:24).

What does the bankruptcy law say about tithing? If you are filing bankruptcy and you give to your church, will you still be able to do so?

A number of years ago it used to be that if you were filing bankruptcy you were not allowed to contribute one cent to your church or charity. The idea was that if you're not paying your debts, you shouldn't be giving money away. They said that if you're tithing, you aren't really the one who is giving. Rather, it's your creditors who are paying your tithes.

I can't tell you how hard that was for me to tell faithful givers that they had to stop tithing while in bankruptcy, sometimes as long as five years. It just seemed like a sacrilege, but the law was the law, and there was no way around it.

Thankfully, one good thing about the major law change in 2005 was that debtors may now contribute up to 15% of their gross income. What a huge swing in the pendulum to go from 0% to 15%. I am so grateful that I can now advise

FORGIVE US OUR DEBTS

my clients that they may keep up their charitable endeavors without fearing negative repercussions from the Court.

I once had a couple who faithfully gave 10% of their income to their church each month. The problem was, they couldn't afford both that and their bills. They were about to lose the roof over their heads because they felt obligated to tithe and because they needed to "save face" with their church leaders. It makes no sense to pay for others to eat when you end up on food stamps or at the food bank. If you are struggling with the issue of how much to give to your church, please pray about it. Then go see your Pastor for guidance. He won't turn you away just because you can't pay. And if he does, maybe you need to find another church!

What is the solution for those who want to give more, but just can't afford to? Perhaps it is a bankruptcy. If you could erase your old credit card bills, loans, medical debts, etc., and straighten out your finances, you could have the financial freedom to contribute generously to your church and other favorite charities again.

God doesn't want your money.
He wants your heart!

Questions for Reflection

1. What are some Bible verses you can think of that discuss tithing?

_____

_____

_____

_____

_____

_____

2. If you are not tithing now, how do you feel about that?

_____

_____

_____

_____

_____

_____

3. Are you giving cheerfully or with pain?

_____

_____

_____

_____

_____

_____

_____

_____

4. Are you serving your debt or are you serving God?

_____

_____

_____

_____

_____

_____

_____

_____

5. If you are tithing now, how does that make you feel? Does it reassure you to know that if you file bankruptcy you may still contribute up to 15% of your gross income to your church?

_____

_____

_____

_____

_____

_____

6. Pray about the amount of money you should give your church each week. Do you believe God can help you contribute that amount? Knowing you are doing God's will, how do you feel?

_____

_____

_____

_____

_____

_____

But who am I,
And who are my people,
That we should be able
To give as generously as this?
Everything comes from you,
And we have given you
Only what comes from your hand.

1 Chronicles 29:14

CHAPTER 4

Bankruptcy and Alternatives for Resolving Debt

YOU KNOW YOU HAVE A FINANCIAL problem, and you know you need to resolve it somehow. Let's talk about what you can do to make things better. The following information is technical and might be boring. Please refer to the chart on the following pages for a quick reference about the different kinds of bankruptcy. If you're interested in more detailed information, keep reading.

There are several options available to help people in financial distress. There are basically four different types of bankruptcy for people to choose from, as well as non-bankruptcy options. The four types of bankruptcy cases are Chapters 7, 11, 12, and Chapter 13.

Below is a chart that summarizes these different types of bankruptcy.

DIFFERENCES IN BANKRUPTCY CHAPTERS

Chapter	
7	**Who Files?** Individuals who need a fresh start now, or corporations going out of business. **Why File?** Chance to start over; stop harassment by bill collectors and creditors; stop lawsuits; erase credit card debt; erase medical debt. **What Kind of Bankruptcy?** Liquidation (auction) of some items sometimes.
Chapter 11	**Who Files?** Corporations staying in business, or individuals with extremely high debt loads (e.g. movie stars, brain surgeons, and those who own multiple houses). **Why File?** Need time to repay bills and restructure how payments will be made; to save business; when debts are too high for individuals in Chapter 13. **What Kind of Bankruptcy?** Reorganization (repayment) of debts over time.

Chapter 12	**Who Files?** Family farmers and fishermen. (Rarely claimed in urban areas.) **Why File?** Need time to catch up bills and save the family farm or commercial fishing business. **What Kind of Bankruptcy?** Reorganization to repay bills.
Chapter 13	**Who Files?** Individuals who need to repay debt when income or assets are too high to file Chapter 7. **Why File?** To save house by catching up past-due payments; to pay back-taxes; to keep property when value is too high for Chapter 7. **What Kind of Bankruptcy?** Wage Earner Plan/Reorganization of individual debt paid over 3 or 5 years.

CHAPTER 12 BANKRUPTCY

Let's start with the type of bankruptcy rarely seen in urban areas of the country, Chapter 12. In the six-county area surrounding Orlando there are very, very few cases filed under Chapter 12. However, Chapter 12 is often used in rural and coastal areas. You see, Chapter 12 is reserved for Family Farmers and Fishermen, and we don't have many of those in the city! Although some people have asked if growing a few tomato plants in the backyard or having an orange tree in the yard counts. No, because you can't be a

"Family Farmer" unless you earn more than 50% of your income from some type of farming or commercial fishing operation. Chapter 12 lets family farmers and fishermen repay their bills over time with their future earnings.

CHAPTER 11 BANKRUPTCY

Chapter 11 is another option where corporations (and sometimes individuals) restructure how they will pay all, or more likely only part, of their debt over time. This complex chapter in bankruptcy is usually used by corporations which are trying to stay in business. Airlines and stores often file Chapter 11 to restructure their debt and stay afloat.

Some individual people file Chapter 11 bankruptcy, but not many. Those people want or need to repay some or all of their debt, but they don't qualify for some of the other types of bankruptcy. Currently, they would not qualify for Chapter 13 unless their unsecured debt is under $394,725 and their secured debt is under $1,184,200. While those amounts seem very high, certain situations arise causing those amounts to kick in.

In the past, very few individuals filed Chapter 11 – usually movie stars and brain surgeons. But now we've seen more Chapter 11 bankruptcies filed by individuals who purchased investment or rental homes in addition to the home they live in. Perhaps they bought one or two houses over the last housing boom, expecting to sell quickly for a profit. Now that the market has changed from a "sellers' market" to a "buyers' market," there aren't enough people in the market to buy the homes. So the investors who thought they'd try their hand at "flipping" a house for a great profit, are now stuck with a 100% financed house that has suddenly become worth less than what they paid for it only months ago. With the cost of houses these days, it's not too hard to be over these Chapter 11 limits if you own more than one home and a couple of cars.

Another situation where people find themselves in Chapter 11 is when they have income and/or assets available to pay some of their debt (so they can't file Chapter 7 discussed below) but their debt is too high to file Chapter 13 (also discussed later in this Chapter). I once represented a businessman who had been involved in litigation for almost four years. He was winning at every stage of the lawsuit, until at the very end, he lost and was required to pay the opposing party's attorney's fees and court costs. This amount was over $400,000, which is over the Chapter 13 debt amount of $394,725 for unsecured debt. Therefore, he was forced to either file Chapter 11 or attempt to negotiate the debt to reach a settlement. (See, Creditor Negotiations, discussed below.)

Most people, however, whether single or married, filing bankruptcy alone or jointly with their spouse, fall into either Chapter 7 or Chapter 13. Chapter 7 has always been the most common Chapter in bankruptcy.

CHAPTER 7 BANKRUPTCY

Chapter 7 is called a "Liquidation." Most of your debts are erased or cancelled within a short period of time, usually less than 6 months. In exchange for a "fresh start," some people in bankruptcy (debtors) are required to give up some property. Some assets owned over and above the allowed amounts (called "exemptions"), may be sold at an auction with the proceeds going to pay down some of the debt. This is why the Chapter 7 is called a "Liquidation," due to the possible liquidating or selling of some of your property to pay some of your debt.

But, don't panic just yet! Most people who file Chapter 7 never have their assets taken away. In fact, most Chapter 7 debtors keep all of their property free and clear and never lose their personal items like clothing, furniture, wedding rings, etc., and even cars. The Chapter 7 discharge erases most debt like credit cards, unsecured loans, medical bills, and old utility bills. However, most taxes, student loans, child support payments, and criminal restitution debts will survive in Chapter 7 bankruptcy. For some people, when they discharge much of their debt, it frees them up so they can start making meaningful payments on their student loans, thus allowing them to actually take care of that non-dischargeable debt once and for all.

So, who files Ch. 7 bankruptcy? People of all ages and all stages file bankruptcy. When I say I have clients from 19 to 90, I'm not kidding! Let me give you some examples of people I've helped in different age groups.

TYLER

Tyler was in his mid-20's when he ran into financial trouble. He lived on his own and worked in maintenance. He didn't earn a lot, but he earned enough to take care of himself. He bought a new-to-him (i.e. "used") truck and financed it at his local credit union. Not long after, however, the engine blew up. It was going to cost $6,000 to repair the truck. He couldn't afford that, so he let the truck go back to the credit union. He owed $20,000 on a truck he didn't even have any more.

Next, he saved up some money to put down on a new motorcycle. He was so proud and thrilled when he drove away that night on his new bike. Unfortunately, on the way home he had an accident. He totaled his new motorcycle and was injured. He was taken by ambulance to the Emergency Room. Thank God he wasn't seriously hurt— just banged up and bruised with only one broken leg. He knew it could have been so much worse.

After the wreck, Tyler was in bad financial trouble. You see, very unwisely, he drove away that fateful night with his new motorcycle without any insurance. He had planned to get it the next day. Too late. His bike was totaled, but he still owed the finance company the full amount he had borrowed.

Also, because he was in an accident with no insurance which caused some property damage to others (only $200 in grass and $200 in damages to a light pole), he was now required by the state to carry special insurance even though he now had no vehicle at all. This insurance cost him $480 per month.

So, Tyler was left with no truck, no motorcycle, very expensive insurance he must pay each month for a year whether or not he has a vehicle, debts to the credit union for the truck and to the finance company for the motorcycle, and medical bills. He needed financial relief in a big way. So, he filed Ch. 7 bankruptcy and was able to wipe out all his debt and start over.

BONNIE

Another example of someone who filed Ch. 7 bankruptcy is Bonnie. She was divorced and lived with her teenage daughter who had medical problems. While her ex-husband did send child support each month, he did not help with any of the medical bills for their daughter.

Every time the daughter had a relapse Bonnie had to miss work to take care of her. She didn't get paid when she didn't work. The bills were piling up for doctors, hospitals, treatment centers, rehabilitation facilities, and counseling.

When her daughter finally stabilized she was able to work steady hours and earn a more stable income. Even though she was no longer incurring more medical bills for her daughter, she realized she could never pay off all the debt. She needed a Ch. 7 bankruptcy.

BANKRUPTCY AND ALTERNATIVES

<u>JOSÉ AND WANDA</u>

Another example of people who filed Ch. 7 bankruptcy is José and Wanda. They are in their 50's. Wanda has a good job. José used to be a professional, but he could no longer work after becoming disabled. He receives a small check for Social Security Disability Income each month.

Over the years the couple had racked up a lot of credit card debt. They never thought much about it because they always paid their minimum payments on time each month. They were getting by, but constantly reaching for the credit cards to fill the gap between José's income and their needs.

Then one day their cousin told them about this great new program she went to and explained how it worked. So, José and Wanda went to a "lunch and learn" seminar at their local Denny's restaurant. They got a free lunch and learned how the IRS "owed" them a lot of money. All they had to do was fill out some papers which gave the promoters 20% of what the IRS paid the couple. In no time they had more than $100,000 in the bank from the IRS. It was a miracle (or so they thought!)

They immediately spent much of the money on home contractors to remodel their home to accommodate José's disability to help him get around the house better. Unfortunately, in the middle of construction Wanda was diagnosed with breast cancer for the third time. While recuperating from surgery and chemotherapy the IRS came calling at home.

This whole "lunch and learn" seminar was nothing but a scam! It didn't take the IRS too long to figure that out, and they wanted the money back now! The IRS garnished their bank accounts. One bank froze the money and returned it to the IRS. But, a second bank failed to freeze the account, and that bank had to pay the IRS a lot of money. Well, it didn't take that bank long to sue the couple to get back the money the bank was required to pay the IRS.

With the IRS closing in on them and the bank refusing to settle the lawsuit for affordable monthly payments, they had no choice but to file Ch. 7 bankruptcy. The IRS debt wasn't going away, but the bank debt, lawsuit, and credit card debt would all be erased.

This just goes to show you that even smart people can fall for a scam. Remember the old saying, "If it sounds too good to be true, it is!"

BILL AND MARCIA

One last example of a couple who filed Ch. 7 bankruptcy is Bill and Marcia. They are in their late 60's and are retired schoolteachers. They needed to move south to be with family when Bill's health started declining. They owned a house up north that they had tried to sell for three years. After burning through their savings, they couldn't keep up with the mortgage payments on the house up north and also pay the rent on their new home down south.

The bank filed a foreclosure lawsuit and threatened a very large deficiency amount they could never repay on their fixed income. They filed Ch. 7 to get out from under the oppressive house debt burden. Bill and Marcia were relieved when the debt was washed away through bankruptcy. They never thought they'd need to file bankruptcy in a million years, but when the old house just wouldn't sell, and the bank sued them, they had no choice.

CHAPTER 13 BANKRUPTCY

The last type of bankruptcy is Chapter 13, which is known as a "Wage Earner Plan" or "Reorganization." It is a restructuring of debt for individuals, like a Chapter 11 is a reorganizing of debt for corporations. In a Chapter 13, all your bills are consolidated into one monthly payment. Instead of making 10 different credit card or loan payments per month, you make one payment into the court to the Chapter 13 Standing Trustee, who administers all the bill repayments to the creditors (people or companies to whom the debt is owed). Creditors are paid back either in full, or usually only partially, over three or five years. At the end of this set period of time, most debt that you weren't able to pay in full will be erased through a discharge, which relieves you of the legal obligation to repay your debts.

Not all debts are completely resolved in Chapter 13. If you haven't paid off your mortgage or car over the three or five-year plan period, you will still need to pay those monthly payments after bankruptcy so you don't lose your house or car. If you don't make your car payments, the bank will repossess the car. If you don't pay your mortgage payments, the lender will foreclose to get the house.

In Chapter 13, the debtor files a repayment "Plan" to repay all or part of their debt out of their future earnings. In the past, as now, most people file Chapter 13 bankruptcy to save their homes from foreclosure. If someone has fallen behind in their mortgage payments, and their bank won't work with them to catch up, they may file a Chapter 13 bankruptcy which will allow them three or five years or catch up the mortgage arrears, while continuing to make their regular monthly mortgage payments.

We also have a streamlined process for Mortgage Modification Mediation which has been very successful in helping people modify their mortgages to get caught up, sometimes with some debt forgiveness, and to get back on track.

Other people file Chapter 13 because they own too much property for Chapter 7 and they don't want to lose any of their assets through a Chapter 7 Liquidation, or auction. As long as they repay the creditors the value of that property over three or five years, they can keep all of their "stuff."

Others file Chapter 13 simply because they want to repay whatever they can on their debt. They feel like they made the debt, so they should pay it. Their consciences won't let them file any type of bankruptcy but a repayment plan through Chapter 13.

Still others file Chapter 13 because they owe a lot of back-taxes to the IRS. A repayment plan stops all the interest and penalties from running which gives the taxpayer a chance to finally pay off the old tax debt. Some people wonder how others can owe so much in taxes when they themselves receive a refund each year. Well, for many it's a matter of owing taxes and penalties on withdrawals of 401(k) money upon the loss of a job. If not enough money was held back, the taxes and penalties due come as a shock with no way to repay. Chapter 13 can help.

Finally, other individuals are forced into Chapter 13 by virtue of the Means Test found within the bankruptcy law. If they make too much money for Chapter 7, even if the money was earned in the past, they may be required to file Chapter 13. The amount you can earn is based on your state's median income for your size family. The Census Bureau amounts change about twice per year, so you'll need to check with an attorney for the most up-to-date numbers. As a practical matter, those who want to file Chapter 7 usually will qualify for it.

KYLE AND KATE

An example of a couple who filed Chapter 13 is Kyle and Kate. They are in their 30's and work for Kyle's parents' small business. They had a 10-year-old and dreamed of a bigger family but that didn't seem to be God's plan for them. Unexpectedly, and happily, Kate was pregnant at long last with their second child. The pregnancy was very difficult, and Kate couldn't work when she was put on early bed rest. The couple fell behind in their mortgage payments. After the baby was born and Kate went back to work, they tried to get a loan modification to catch up the back payments. No luck. They tried a second time and then a third. Each time the bank denied their request.

They filed Chapter 13 to save their home and it worked! They are now making monthly payments inside a Chapter 13 repayment plan and will be completely caught up and current in their mortgage payments when their plan is completed in five years.

Kyle and Kate are blessed to be expecting their third child next month. This time there have been no complications. They couldn't be happier knowing they made a great decision to file bankruptcy to save their home for their growing family.

LIZ AND FRANK

Another example of people in a Chapter 13 bankruptcy is Liz and Frank. Liz has a good steady job. Frank, who works in construction management, has suffered bouts of unemployment over the years. They are in their 50's with two kids in college. Frank earns a lot of money – when he works. The problem is once he completes a project he is laid off. His time between jobs has added up, and the couple has lived on credit cards to make ends meet in between his jobs.

Frank has finally found a good permanent job – but the bills have just piled up with no way to pay them off at 18%, 22% or 32% interest. So, they filed Chapter 13 bankruptcy to repay as much as they can. With their high income they couldn't pass the Means Test to file Chapter 7. Also, they wanted to repay what they could. Now, with credit cards being paid back at 0% interest instead of 32%, they are making huge strides in repaying debt. In 60 months, they'll be debt free!

RICHARD

One more example of someone who filed Chapter 13 is Richard. He is a widower in his 90's. Yes, you read that correctly.

Richard worked his whole life and his wife stayed home and paid all the bills. He was an engineer for a large company and always made a good living. When he retired, he received a nice pension each month in addition to his Social Security check. After his wife died, he discovered that she had run up more than $50,000 in credit card debt which was in both of their names. He had no idea he was in debt.

Due to his pension he could afford to pay some of the bills back, just not in the amounts the creditors wanted. So, he filed Chapter 13 bankruptcy. Because he receives less money than the Florida Median Income, we were able to design a plan for him to repay some of his debt in just three years. Richard will become debt free at age 94! Better late than never! Also, he is glad he won't leave a mess behind for his sons to sort out later.

LEGAL VS. MORAL OBLIGATION

The Discharge which comes at the end of your case relieves you of the legal obligation to repay debts. However, there is a difference between a legal and a moral obligation. Some people hate the idea of discharging a debt owed to their father or sister. But, I tell them that if they feel a moral obligation to repay their family, they are certainly welcome to repay the family in the future as they are able. No law stops someone from doing what is right and important to them as far as taking care of these perceived moral obligations. In addition, if someone wins the lottery five years after bankruptcy, although they have no legal obligation to repay all the debts discharged previously in bankruptcy, they may voluntarily repay every penny owed.

As a practical matter, an old creditor may not accept a payment on a debt written off years before. In that case, a person who wants to fulfill a moral obligation or feels they need to repay their debt to society with their new found good fortune, may want to "pay it forward." By this I mean, make a nice donation to your favorite church or other charity. You could even help a family in need you know of.

Many, many years ago my husband and I were really struggling financially. My husband had his pay cut three times in one year, and I was not being paid at work either. I confided in one of my friends for moral support – not seeking any money. She was so moved that she later wrote me a check for $300 and called it "pizza money." I have never forgotten this great act of kindness. She did not want to be repaid ever. So, after we recovered financially, I learned of another friend at church who was suffering her own financial misfortune. I was able to "pay it forward" by giving her money with no strings attached. It felt so good to be able to bless someone after I had been blessed.

NON-BANKRUPTCY OPTIONS

What about non-bankruptcy options? What can a person do when they don't have too much debt, or they just can't face the idea of actually filing bankruptcy?

CREDIT COUNSELING

Sometimes bankruptcy isn't necessary, or advisable. Sometimes, credit counseling through a reputable, nonprofit agency can help. The agency might be able to negotiate with your creditors in order to reduce the interest rate and/or the amount paid monthly to each creditor. Then, you pay the credit counselor one lump sum per month through a Debt Management Plan or "DMP". (A DMP is similar to a Chapter 13 bankruptcy repayment plan; however, in a Chapter 13 all interest on unsecured debt like credit cards drops to zero percent, and late fees and over-the-limit fees are all stopped.) For people who don't have too much debt compared to their income, a DMP may be the way to go to resolve their financial woes. **Caution** should be exercised in choosing a credit counselor, however, as many people have become victims of unscrupulous companies that keep their payments as a "fee" without paying down the debts.

Instead of DMP's, some people go to companies that say they will negotiate lump sum payments with creditors. You send in a monthly payment, and instead of the agency paying your bills each month, they stockpile the money (usually including a lot for their fees). After you've sent in so much money, the agency will attempt to negotiate a one-time lump sum for one debt. Then, you keep sending in money and they try to negotiate to pay off another debt. The problem with this method, however, is that while the agency is saving your money, you are being charged late fees, and interest on top of interest. Your prior balance is growing exponentially while little headway is being made toward reducing the debt. **I don't ever recommend this type of "credit counseling" because I've never seen it work.**

CREDITOR NEGOTIATIONS

Finally, other than hitting the lottery or inheriting millions from your long lost great uncle, the other option to filing bankruptcy is to do what I call "Creditor Negotiations." This usually requires you to obtain a good size sum of money, usually at least one-half of the amount of the debt you want to take care of. Perhaps you have a family member who is willing and able to help you out. Or, maybe you want to cash in an annuity or a life insurance policy (which is not required under the law in Florida). Maybe you even want to sell the house you've owned for ten years and use some of the proceeds to pay towards your debt. (Again, in Florida you would almost never be required to sell your house to pay off your bills.)

So let's say you can gather a lump sum of cash one way or the other, but you don't have enough to pay everyone in full. What I like to do under those circumstances, is send a letter to all your creditors advising them that I'm a bankruptcy attorney and that my client would prefer not to file bankruptcy. I inquire as to whether the creditor would be willing to settle the debt for a smaller amount than the full amount owed.

It often takes a very long time to settle with creditors through their representatives. It can take a year or more to settle, whereas a Chapter 7 bankruptcy is generally much quicker. It seems that with these large credit card companies the "left hand doesn't know what the right hand is doing." My settlement letters float from one department to the next until the right person finally responds. Usually, once the person in a position to settle comes forward, they want to settle quickly, trying to meet their end of the month collection quotas. That's why it's essential to have the settlement money ready to go. I usually require the money to be held in my attorney Trust Account so there is no question of the availability of funds.

Creditor Negotiations can be an effective way to resolve debt problems. However, it requires a lot of patience over time, and can be more expensive than filing bankruptcy in terms of attorney's fees and the cost to pay off your debts.

When creditors won't work with you, or when your debt is just too high to manage, bankruptcy may be the best option available. The bankruptcy law is tricky, so it's important to consult with a qualified bankruptcy attorney in your state to determine the best course of action in your specific and unique situation.

Let the wise listen
and add to their learning,
and let the discerning
get guidance.

Proverbs 1:5

Questions for Reflection

1. Chapter 7 bankruptcy has a scary name, "Liquidation." Are you afraid you will lose everything if you file bankruptcy? Are you afraid they will take your wedding ring, clothes, and furniture? Write down what you are afraid of. Then you can discuss each item with a qualified bankruptcy attorney who can give you good legal advice based on your particular situation. Replace fear with facts!

---

2. In a Chapter 13 bankruptcy, you will repay some of your debt over three or five years. Are you afraid the payments will be more than you can afford? What else are you worried about with a possible Chapter 13 repayment plan? Write down all your concerns so they can be addressed by a competent bankruptcy attorney who is there to help you.

_____

_____

_____

_____

_____

_____

3. Do you understand there is a difference between a legal obligation and a moral obligation when it comes to repaying debt? If you "hit the lottery" would you repay your debt? Would you help others in need?

_____

_____

_____

_____

_____

4. If you borrowed money from a family member, will you repay them in the future when you are able, even though you are no longer legally required to do so? How do you feel about moral obligations?

_____

_____

_____

_____

5. Credit Counseling and Creditor Negotiations can also be ways to resolve financial problems. How do you feel knowing you have other alternatives available?

_____

_____

_____

_____

6. Are you willing to openly and honestly discuss your complete financial situation with an attorney who can help you find the best solution for you in your personal circumstances?

_____

_____

If you are interested in learning about your financial options in your specific situation, call my office at 407-228-1300 or send an email to office@bowenbankruptcylaw.com and mention you saw this Special Offer in Forgive Us Our Debts.

I normally charge $375/hour.* **When you mention this Special Offer, I will provide you with up to one hour of a personalized initial consultation *for only $100*.**

That's a *huge* savings to get information that specifically applies to you and that can help you gain some peace of mind.

Plus, your $100 discounted initial consultation fee will be applied to your full flat attorney's fees should you chose to move forward with filing bankruptcy within 30 days of the consultation.

CALL NOW 407-228-1300

OR EMAIL office@bowenbankruptcylaw.com for your Special Offer.

Please note, I am licensed to practice law in Florida only.

· CHAPTER 5 ·

Biblical Authority for Bankruptcy

MANY CHRISTIANS FEEL SO CONFLICTED about filing bankruptcy. They wonder if it is moral to do so.

We are told in Romans 13:1 to obey the law. "Let everyone be subject to the governing authorities, for there is no authority except that which God has established. The authorities that exist have been established by God." (Romans 13:1). The authority is the law, and the law says that bankruptcy is legal. (See Title 11 U.S. Code – Bankruptcy). Because Scripture says it is okay to file bankruptcy, and the law allows it, you should feel free to do so if it is appropriate in your circumstances.

Article I, Section 8, of the United States Constitution specifies that Congress shall have the power to establish "uniform laws on the subject of bankruptcies throughout the United States." It is pretty amazing that back in 1787 when our founding fathers wrote the Constitution, they specifically singled out bankruptcy laws among so many other topics that could have been included. Our founders had been living under the oppressive English legal system which still employed debtor's prisons for those unable to repay their debt. I believe these great men of old felt it necessary to protect their citizens by providing for the establishment of bankruptcy laws which could resolve financial burdens by means other than going to prison when poor souls could not repay their debts.

BANKRUPTCY MIRRORS THE BIBLE

Chapter 7

There are multiple examples of the bankruptcy laws mirroring the Bible. In the Old Testament we see that every seven years the debts are forgiven (See, Deuteronomy 15:1-2). In Chapter 7 bankruptcy, for many, many years until 2005, a person could file Chapter 7 bankruptcy and erase his debt once every seven years. (Now it's every eight years.)

Chapter 13

Chapter 13 also reflects Biblical principles in that debtors are required to repay their debts out of their future earnings over a three or five-year repayment period. At the end of this time, most debts are forgiven. This is similar to debtors in ancient times being required to repay their debt for a set period of time (seven years), and then having the debts cancelled at the end of the repayment period.

DEBTORS NOT TO BE LEFT EMPTY-HANDED

There are multiple examples in the Bible where a debtor is not permitted to be left completely empty-handed such that he would perish. For instance, Exodus 22:26 says that if a creditor takes his neighbor's cloak as a pledge (i.e. collateral for repayment of a loan), the lender must "return it by sunset, because that cloak is the only covering your neighbor has. What else can they sleep in?" Thus, God didn't want people to freeze to death without their cloaks to cover them at night.

Deuteronomy 24:6 (NASB) provides,

No one shall take a handmill or an upper millstone in pledge, for he would be taking a life in pledge.

In other words, a lender could not take a handmill as collateral for a loan because the Israelites ground their grain into flour with this tool. They only ground enough for their current needs, such that if a creditor took the mill, the debtor would starve to death as he would have no way to turn his grain into flour. God did not want people and their families to starve to death just because they could not repay a loan.

Finally, Deuteronomy 15:12-14 discusses what happens when slaves are set free in the seventh year.

> *When you release them,*
> *do not send them away empty-handed.*
> *Supply them liberally from your flock,*
> *your threshing floor and your winepress.*

God wanted people to be able to start their new life in freedom with food, drink, and animals so they could live.

EXEMPTIONS

This idea of starting over with something rather than nothing is mirrored in our bankruptcy laws under something called "Exemptions." Exemptions are the things the law says debtors may keep in spite of declaring bankruptcy, possessions which are exempt from seizure.

There are federal exemptions and each state also has its own exemption laws. If you have lived in the state of Florida for more than two years at the time you file bankruptcy here, you are entitled to keep the equity in your homestead up to a certain dollar limit, or possibly in an unlimited amount, depending on when you purchased the home. You may claim as exempt property $1,000 worth of personal property (furniture, clothing, jewelry, etc.); all your retirement savings (IRA's, 401(k)'s, pensions); cash value of life insurance and annuities you own; $1,000 towards equity in one motor vehicle. If you do not claim a homestead exemption, you are entitled to an additional $4,000 to go towards any personal property you want to keep. This $4,000 is called the "Wildcard Exemption."

Exemptions vary greatly state to state, and claiming exemptions can be quite complicated. You really need an attorney to do this correctly. Note that there are other exemptions available which I have not mentioned above as it is beyond the scope of this book. The point is that just as in Biblical times when people were not to be sent away empty-handed, in modern times, people will not leave bankruptcy Court empty-handed either. Thus, exemption laws are one more example where bankruptcy laws mirror the Bible.

REDEMPTION

In both the Old Testament and the New Testament, we read a lot about redemption. But what does it mean to redeem? The dictionary says it means to set free; rescue; to save from sin; to recover ownership of by paying a specified sum. Deuteronomy and Leviticus talk of people and their property being redeemed, or being bought back at a set price. We hear that God redeemed His people from slavery multiple times.

In the New Testament we hear of the ultimate sacrifice of redemption - - Christ died for our sins, our debt is repaid through the grace of God. "In him we have redemption through his blood, the forgiveness of sins, in accordance with the riches of God's grace." (Ephesians 1:7).

Similar to the concept of redemption in the Bible, we have redemption codified in the U.S. Bankruptcy Code. This is the availability to pay off a secured debt at today's fair market value instead of the full amount owed.

Let me tell you about Jim and his car, by way of example. Jim, had filed a Chapter 7 Bankruptcy case. He owed $20,000 on his old car that was only worth $7,000. The finance company had a lien on his title so if Jim did not make his car payments, the bank would repossess the car. But, did it really make sense for Jim to pay $20,000 at 14% interest on a car worth only $7,000? Over time, Jim would end up paying close to $30,000 for a car worth closer to $5,000.

I told Jim about redemption under the bankruptcy law. Jim could redeem his car by paying the bank today's fair market value (i.e. $7,000) rather than the full amount he owed ($20,000). The "catch" is that he had to pay the $7,000 in a lump sum. So Jim could either cash in some retirement money, borrow from a family member, or even finance the $7,000 with another lender. (Believe it or not, there are companies that help debtors refinance the amount of their old car debt in the middle of a bankruptcy case.)

Jim gathered the funds, we petitioned the court, and the deal went through. Jim was very happy to now be paying only what the car was worth, rather than three times its value. This helped him get on his feet and not be overburdened with too much debt relative to the value of the collateral. He then had lower, reasonable monthly car payments he could afford.

Although Christians are often conflicted about bankruptcy, we know we are to follow the law. We also know bankruptcy is legal, as established at the beginning of our country. Finally, we see bankruptcy laws reflect the principles of the Bible in various ways such as forgiveness of debt, repayment of debt over a set period of time, property kept after the bondage of debt is released (i.e. exemptions), and redemption. My dear Christian brothers and sisters, allow yourselves and your debt to be redeemed and forgiven "in accordance with the riches of God's grace." (Ephesians 1:7).

*Israel, put your hope in the Lord,
for with the Lord is unfailing love
and with him is full redemption.*

Psalm 130:7

Questions for Reflection

1. Have you felt conflicted about your possible need to file bankruptcy? Have you wondered whether it is moral to do so?

_____

_____

_____

_____

_____

2. What do you think about the Bible telling you to obey governing authorities?

_____

_____

_____

_____

_____

3. Are you surprised that one of the few things specifically enumerated when our country was formed concerned bankruptcy law?

_____

_____

_____

_____

_____

_____

_____

2. How do you feel knowing the bankruptcy law mirrors the Bible in terms of a set repayment period and then a time of forgiveness of debt?

_____

_____

_____

_____

_____

_____

_____

5. The Bible is clear that debtors will not be left empty-handed. Likewise, the Bankruptcy law specifies what real and personal property a debtor may keep after bankruptcy. Describe how you may be comforted knowing if you must go through bankruptcy, you will still have something and not lose everything like "the shirt off your back"?

_____

_____

_____

_____

_____

_____

_____

6. Read Ephesians 1:7. How do you feel knowing Christ died for our sins and our debt is repaid through the Grace of God?

_____

_____

_____

_____

_____

_____

CHAPTER 6

Broken and Blessed on the Journey

ON THE JOURNEY OF LIFE WE ALL undertake, things don't always go as planned. In fact, probably a lot of times things don't go as planned. What's the old saying? "If you want to make God laugh, tell Him your plans!" Some people call it Murphy's Law. Whatever you call it, it happens to all of us at various times in our lives and to varying degrees.

MARIA AND LOUIS

Maria and Louis came to see me a while back. They were a hardworking couple who had done their best to provide for their kids. They went to work every day, made sure their kids did their homework each night, got the kids to baseball practice and games on time, and went to church without fail each week. They were busy but happy.

Then one day everything changed. Maria was laid off from her job of ten years when her company got into trouble with the IRS and was shut down without warning.

At the same time, Louis hurt his back while helping a friend move. He was in such pain that he could no longer work as a deliveryman loading cases of soda in and out of his truck all day.

The couple started living on credit cards, because that was the only way they could make it. With three kids, they didn't have a lot saved.

Louis was visiting various doctors, specialists, clinics, and labs searching for relief from his severe back pain. They ran up medical bills without even trying. You see, when they lost their jobs, they lost their health insurance, too. They could not see any way out of their situation which was spinning out of control.

Eventually Maria got another job, but she was paid less than her old job where she had worked for a decade. Starting a new job meant she was starting over, pay wise. Louis wasn't working and didn't know what he was going to do.

By the time they came to see me, Maria and Louis had used up all their savings, had maxed out their credit cards, had incurred loans, and medical bills, and were out of resources. They were surrounded by the darkness of debt, and the only light they could see at the end of the tunnel seemed to be a train headed straight for them.

During our initial consultation, Maria shed tears of sadness and frustration. She said, "I just don't understand. I've prayed and prayed for deliverance, but I just don't see a way out." They were both so ashamed to even be considering filing bankruptcy. They felt like God abandoned them because He didn't answer their prayers the way they wanted and in their timeframe.

Now, you and I know that God doesn't always do what we want when we want Him to. "Thy Will be done" is the prayer - not "my will be done." But when you are the one in the midst of a giant struggle you don't always see things clearly and remember what you've been taught.

Remember Moses leading the Israelites through the dessert for 40 years? They wandered aimlessly, grumbled against God, but always repented after punishment. They may not have seen the promised land due to their rebellion against God, but their children did make it to the land of milk and honey.

Deuteronomy 2:7 says:

> *The Lord your God has blessed you*
> *in all the work of your hands.*
> *He has watched over your journey*
> *through this vast wilderness.*
> *These forty years*
> *the Lord your God has been with you,*
> *and you have not lacked anything.*

When the Israelites were hungry, God provided manna from Heaven. It wasn't steak or prime rib, but it was food to nourish them. They did not starve to death in the desert.

When they were thirsty, God had Moses strike a rock and water poured forth. It wasn't a Coke, sweet tea, or other favorite beverage, but it hydrated them well. They did not die of thirst in the wilderness.

PERSONAL DIFFICULTIES

Recently, I've experienced some great challenges in my own family. My precious mother who was struggling with heart problems for a few years died after a long journey of declining health. After her last hospital stay, the doctors sent her home to die. It was a difficult seven weeks until she breathed her last breath.

I was exhausted from helping with the physical needs of my dying mom, and the emotional needs of my poor 90-year-old dad struggling with losing his wife of 67 years.

Thank God my parents' old Pastor happened to be in town for a meeting. He had moved up North a couple of years ago, and as a family friend, I texted him to let him know how grave the situation was, and to ask him to call Dad to give him some comfort. Pastor Joe did not reply. Instead, he unexpectedly showed up on their doorstep.

He was able to minister to my parents, pray over my mom, and pray with us. As he was leaving, I walked him out to his car. I told him of some very unpleasant words one of my relatives had said about the alleged lack of faith she saw. Pastor Joe was surprised and said, "I see nothing but faith in this house." He said that God didn't say we wouldn't have troubles, and sorrow, and grief. But he did say He would walk with us - - He would not abandon us.

Even though we believe in everlasting life, it doesn't mean we aren't human. We have real human emotions. We experience pain and loss. Even Jesus wept when his friend Lazarus died. When someone is dying, we don't have to be joyfully shouting, "Halleluiah," to have faith. We are human beings, and our pain is real.

TOUGH CHALLENGES LEAD TO BROKENNESS

When you are faced with losing your house, or car, or health, or job, or anything else of value, it is hard. But God will never forsake or abandon you. (Hebrews 13:5). We have to go through the process and face our burdens with hope. Life is hard, but God is good!

Many times when people endure financial reversals, they feel broken. They are embarrassed and feel like a failure, whether whatever happened to them was their fault or not. Often what led to their financial problems was a combination of poor spending choices and outside factors beyond their control.

People often think they are doing fine financially when they pay their bills and minimum payments on time each month. But, someone who lives paycheck to paycheck can easily get into trouble. When a hurricane blows through town and your employer is without power for five days, that means you aren't working and consequently aren't getting paid for nearly a week. For a lot of people, missing these days or hours of work is devastating.

WORRY AND FEAR

We worry so much, but God tells us not to. He tells us not to be afraid, but we are.

Jesus said in Luke 12:22-24,

Therefore I tell you,
do not worry about your life,
what you will eat; or about your body,
what you will wear.

For life is more than food,
and the body more than clothes.

Consider the ravens:
They do not sow or reap,
they have no storeroom or barn;
yet God feeds them.

And how much more valuable
you are than birds!

God knows what we need even before we do. God will always do His part, but we need to do our part, too. Often that entails gathering information, instead of just worrying. It involves reaching out for help, instead of just being afraid.

Ask and it will be given to you;
seek and you will find; knock
and the door will be opened to you.

Luke 11:9

BROKEN AND BLESSED

You may feel broken now, but open your hearts, and you will be blessed. Sometimes we suffer great disappointments, but later we discover a great blessing has come out of this disappointment. Maybe you have to go through what seems like financial ruin and upheaval, so that you can later help someone in need.

Since he himself has gone through
suffering and testing,
he is able to help us
when we are being tested.

Hebrews 2:18 (NLT)

You'll understand, having walked in their shoes. You can be a beacon of hope for another. So, as you endure your own suffering, remember that God is with you on this journey called life!

We know that suffering
produces perseverance;
perseverance, character;
and character, hope.
And hope does not put us to shame,
because God's love has been poured out
into our hearts through the Holy Spirit,
who has been given to us.

Romans 5:3-5

Questions for Reflection

1. Think of a time when you were younger, and things didn't go the way you hoped. Maybe the guy you wanted to date asked out your best friend instead of you. Or maybe you didn't make the team. Or maybe you didn't get the class you needed to graduate early. Describe your memories in detail.

_____

_____

_____

_____

_____

2. After you lived through this disappointment, did you survive? Did you thrive? Did you end up with something even better than what you had wanted? What lesson did you learn from this experience?

_____

_____

_____

_____

3. "Thy will be done." "Not what I want, but what God wants for me." How does this make you feel? Do you feel helpless? Or, do you feel comforted to know that it's not all up to you?

_____

_____

_____

_____

_____

_____

_____

4. Read Hebrews 13:5. Do you believe that God will never abandon you? As you look back on prior bad times in your life, how did God help you get through it?

_____

_____

_____

_____

_____

_____

5. Read Luke 12:22-24. What are you worried about that God can't help you with? Nothing, right?! So, write down your worries and fears now.

_____

_____

_____

_____

_____

_____

_____

6. Reflect on how you might be broke and broken now, but blessed in the future. When have you suffered a disappointment and later realized it was a blessing in disguise?

_____

_____

_____

_____

_____

· CHAPTER 7 ·

Slavery, Service, and Grace

THERE ARE MANY, MANY REFERENCES in the Bible to money and possessions. Crown Ministries – a 12-week Bible Study about finances offered at churches throughout the world – teaches that there are more than 2,350 verses in the Bible about handling money, while there are only about 500 verses on prayer, and less than 500 verses on faith. God must have known how much of our lives would revolve around money, because He had quite a lot to say about it.

Romans is clear in the command that we should "owe nothing to anyone." (Romans 13:8 (NASB)). Yet we all do.

Proverbs is full of admonitions about debt. Proverbs 22:7 explains why we don't want to be in debt:

The rich rule over the poor, and the borrower is slave to the lender.

This is exactly what I see in my law practice. The "rich" being the credit card companies, banks, and lenders, ruling over the "poor", or the people in debt, with ever increasing interest rates.

When people have such overwhelming debt, they often spend a good deal of their time figuring out how they will pay their bills. It takes an enormous effort, a lot of energy and worry, to keep the "wolves at bay." When I see the tired faces with worry lines on their foreheads, I'll tell Christians that when you are a slave to debt, you aren't free to serve the Lord.

People struggling with debt can't give 100% effort to their Bible study, to their weekly worship service, or to a group they might be called upon to serve. They can't hear the "call" over the constant ringing of the telephone. They spend their time beating themselves up about how they let debt and the devil take over their lives or lamenting over the tragedies which have struck them. They can't see the "forest" of everlasting life through the "trees" of distraction and distress.

Many years ago, one of our bankruptcy Trustees (who I'm sure would not want their name used here for modesty, humility, and in keeping with the image of a strong Trustee) told me one of the best pieces of advice I could ever give any Christian client. You won't hear me say this every day, only when prompted by the Holy Spirit. And here is my version of this beautiful truth…

Filing bankruptcy is like experiencing Salvation right here on earth.
You made this debt,
you owe this money and should have to pay it all back.
But for the Grace of God through the bankruptcy law, you won't have to repay all the debt under such oppressive terms.

St. Paul in his letter to the Ephesians says,

But because of his great love for us,
God, who is rich in mercy,
made us alive with Christ even
when we were dead in transgressions –
it is by grace you have been saved.

Ephesians 2:4-5

In Ephesians, we learn more about our need to serve others.

For we are God's handiwork,
created in Christ Jesus to do good works,
which God prepared in advance
for us to do.

Ephesians 2:10

God saves us so that we are free to do His good works and to live in those good works as God's own handiwork. God doesn't want to see His children chained in the slavery of debt. He freely gives us the gift of salvation. Say "yes" and it is yours – no strings (or chains) attached!

No one can serve two masters. Either
you will hate the one and love the other,
or you will be devoted to the one and
despise the other. You cannot serve both
God and money.

Matthew 6:24

So stop serving your debt and start serving your Lord!

We don't live in ancient times when there were Jubilee years or Sabbatical years when all the slaves were set free and debts were forgiven. (See Leviticus 25 and Deuteronomy 15). But we also don't have "debtor's prisons" anymore where people are thrown in prison, usually left to die, if they cannot pay their debt.

What we do have is the bankruptcy law. It's not perfect. It's not always fair. It's a lot of work to file correctly so as to obtain relief, but relief is indeed available for those who need it and who are willing to accept the gift of grace from God.

Accept God's grace.
Stop serving your debt
And start serving your Lord!

Questions for Reflection

1. There are more verses in the Bible on money and possessions than most other topics like prayer and faith. How do you feel knowing God knew we'd have struggles with money?

_____

_____

_____

_____

_____

_____

2. How do you feel about being in debt when you know the Bible says not to? Do you feel like a slave to your debt?

_____

_____

_____

_____

_____

_____

3. Are you distracted by your financial problems? Are you unable to serve your neighbor and God because you're busy serving your debt?

_____

_____

_____

_____

_____

_____

4. Read Ephesians 2:4-5. Are you ready to accept God's Grace? Will you open your heart and mind to seek the help you need to resolve your financial problems?

_____

_____

_____

_____

_____

_____

5. Consider Matthew 6:24. What is this verse saying to you about serving two masters?

_____

_____

_____

_____

_____

_____

_____

6. We don't live in times of debtor's prisons, but we also don't have Jubilee or Sabbatical years as in the Old Testament days. However, we do have bankruptcy laws and alternatives. How do you feel about learning more about what you can do to reverse your financial predicament?

_____

_____

_____

_____

_____

_____

CHAPTER 8

Life Lessons from Bankruptcy

BANKRUPTCY CAN BE A VERY teachable moment in time in your life. This is one of the reasons I love my calling as a bankruptcy attorney. It is so very rewarding to help people through one of the most difficult periods of their lives and to shepherd them to a better way of doing things. To offer hope for their future. To help them examine the past so that it is not repeated.

EXAMINE YOUR FINANCIAL LIFE

You need to carefully review your own situation. What happened that caused you to need to file bankruptcy? For many people there may have been a life event which they had no control over. Maybe it was a job loss, death of a spouse, divorce, or illness. People who have savings and no debt going into an unexpected tragedy, may not end up in bankruptcy.

Many people think they have no financial problems at all because they can afford their payments. But if their employer cuts out all overtime, or cuts their weekly hours, they may not be able to make all the payments on time.

You have to ask yourself whether you used credit cards irresponsibly? Did you buy things you didn't need? What do you have to show for the $20,000 or $50,000 or more in credit card debt you've accumulated? Most people have no idea what they bought so many charges ago over so much time.

Are you a shopaholic? Do you go to the store and spend money to make yourself feel better? If so, recognize that a new shirt or outfit may feel great when you buy it that day, but it won't feel so good when the bill comes in.

Maybe you're not a shopaholic *per se*, but you're a serial shopper. Everyday you stop at 7-11 for a Coke, or Walgreens for a few things. Or you're a "cereal" shopper, as in you stop at the grocery store every day for "just one thing." You know good and well you'll find something else to buy while you're there. So plan to grocery shop only once per week. Make a list and stick to it. If it's not on the shopping list, don't buy it – you don't need it.

The reason I'm suggesting you examine your situation carefully is so that you don't repeat past mistakes. Determine what bad financial decisions you made in the past so you can avoid these same mistakes in the future.

"NO" IS NOT A FOUR-LETTER WORD

Some people just need to learn to say "No." I've had multiple cases where a parent, or even a grandparent, ends up in bankruptcy because they did not say "No" to their adult children or grandchildren.

Sue, a darling lady with a heart of gold, found herself in a huge pile of trouble. She agreed to let her unmarried, pregnant granddaughter move in with her after Sue's husband died. She figured it would be a win-win. Sue would have company and the granddaughter would have a roof over her head. Well, it wasn't long before grandma was letting her granddaughter use her credit cards whenever she wanted. Baby needs diapers, no problem. Need clothes, no problem. Need a car to get to work (when she had no job), no problem, grandma will co-sign with you or buy it for you, hoping you'll make the payments. (Like that's going to happen…) When the granddaughter stopped making payments, the car was repossessed and grandma was sued for the deficiency balance due.

Incidentally, they say that 85% of the time when someone co-signs a loan, they are called on to make the payments. Why such a high statistic? Because lenders recognize the borrowers' odds of repayment are slim. Lenders require a co-signer to take the risk. So, say "No" and don't risk it!

Also, sometimes you need to say "No" to yourself. Delayed gratification is not a bad thing. Some say it even builds character.

TEACH YOUR KIDS

Maybe your parents didn't teach you the first thing about how to handle money. But you can and should teach your own children. Don't pretend nothing happened. If you have teenagers, it is okay to tell them you filed bankruptcy. Help them understand what happened so they don't end up in the same situation.

When your son wants a $200 pair of new athletic shoes, it's okay to tell him you can't afford it. It's also okay to tell him that if he wants them, he can go earn his own money to buy them. What a great time to teach him a lesson about "needs" versus "wants". He may need athletic shoes, but he doesn't need the most expensive, latest greatest shoes, especially when the ones he has now will do nicely.

FINANCIAL EDUCATION

As part of the bankruptcy process, you must take a class to get into bankruptcy and a class to get out of bankruptcy. The first class takes one hour and it basically says you're poor so you need to file bankruptcy, and here's your certificate. The second course is two hours long and people may actually learn something. They talk about interest rates, the true cost of money, saving, etc. So these two required classes are a start, but only a small start in learning more about personal finances.

I want to encourage you to learn some basic financial skills that can really help you in the future. Consider attending Dave Ramsey's Financial Peace University, or Crown Ministry or another financial course in your church. Listen to Dave Ramsey, Clark Howard, and Ric Edelman on the radio. Read their books as they are quite enlightening and educational. Clark Howard has a large assortment of great materials and blogs at Clark.com. He calls himself the "Consumer Warrior" and wants to help you "save more, spend less, and avoid getting ripped off." Dave Ramsey and his wife filed bankruptcy about 30 years ago and have made it their life's work to help others avoid it. Dave talks about "debt is dumb, cash is king, and the new status symbol is the paid for car."

ATTITUDE

Now is a good time to re-think your attitude about money and possessions. You may need a car. You don't necessarily need the one you're driving with the high car payments. You don't necessarily need a new car every 3 – 5 years either.

You need a roof over your head. But you don't necessarily need the house you currently live in. You don't have to own a new house when renting for a while works just fine.

Also, think about whether you might consciously or unconsciously succumb to peer pressure even though you're an adult. Did keeping up with the Joneses contribute to your financial mess? If so, let it go. Stop it! Don't worry about what others think about the car you drive or the clothes you wear. (See Luke 12:24).

FRESH START

Bankruptcy attorneys often say, "Get a Fresh Start." After bankruptcy, you get a chance to start your financial life over. It's a chance for a "do-over." As adults, we don't get many chances for that, but this is one.

Your bankruptcy Discharge gives you a chance to make better choices in the future. You now have opportunities going forward that you didn't have when you were forever struggling with debt. When you've made it through the bankruptcy process, learn your lessons well, teach others, and give thanks.

Questions for Reflection

1. Describe in detail what happened that contributed to your current financial situation.

_____

_____

_____

_____

_____

_____

2. Have you fallen behind in payments to your creditors? If so, why? When was the first time you missed a payment? What happened at that time? How did you feel?

_____

_____

_____

_____

_____

3. What can you do differently in the future to prevent your past mistakes?

_____

_____

_____

4. Do you have a hard time saying "No" to others? To yourself?

_____

_____

5. Are you willing to teach your kids / grandkids how to handle money so they don't end up with financial problems?

_____

_____

6. What is the most important thing you have learned on this financial journey?

_____

_____

_____

7. What steps will you take to continue your own personal financial education?

_____

_____

_____

_____

_____

8. What are you grateful for today?

_____

_____

_____

_____

_____

_____

_____

_____

_____

_____

For I have learned to be content in
whatever circumstances I am.
I know how to get along
with humble means,
and I also know how to live
in prosperity;

In any and every circumstance
I have learned
the secret of being filled
and going hungry,
both of having abundance
and suffering need.

I can do all things through him who
strengthens me.

Philippians 4:11-13 (NASB)

CHAPTER 9

Financial Tips for your Future

THERE is an old bankruptcy saying: "There's two solutions to your problem. You either need more income or less expenses!" This is said in jest; but, it is actually pretty true when it comes right down to it. The following are some practical tips, and Do's and Don'ts, to help you as you get your finances in order so you can have a better financial future.

SHOPPING

People spend a <u>lot</u> of money at the grocery store. It's very easy to toss things into those big carts. There are a lot of products you can buy at the grocery store that aren't even food, such as expensive toiletries, kitchen gadgets, pet supplies, batteries, etc. These are items you can find cheaper some place else.

It's easy to spend more than you plan to when you pay with plastic. So, use cash, and you'll know how much you're paying before you check out. You won't throw extra items into your cart when you know you have to hand over cold hard cash.

Buy only what you need when you need it. Don't buy 50 bottles of vitamins because they're a good price. They'll go bad by the time you go to use them, or you'll forget you bought them when they are sitting in the back of your cabinet.

Don't shop at the Big Box Clubs. You spend way too much money. Every item you buy is a minimum of $10. Do you really need 500 tall kitchen garbage bags at once? If you use two bags per week, you have almost 5 years' worth of bags on hand! Is that really necessary?

If you do shop at the Big Box Clubs, then don't shop with a giant shopping cart. It's too easy to put things in that cart. If you have to walk around the store carrying what you're purchasing that day, you will spend less money. Do you really need 10 giant containers of peanuts when you're the only one in your house who eats them? Won't they be stale by the time you get to the last container?

BANKING

One place people waste a lot of money is the bank. So many people bank at large national banks and pay $10 - $15 a month in service fees if they don't have a very high balance on hand. $15 a month times 12 months is $180 a year. Over ten years, that's $1,800. Why pay all those service fees if you don't have to?

Switch banks and go to your local credit union. Most credit unions only require you to maintain a $5 or $10 balance in a savings account. Some people think they can't use a credit union because they're not members of a certain group. That's not usually the case today. For example, our local teacher's credit union used to require you to work for the school system to become a member. Now, if you live, work, or worship in the county, you can be a member.

CELL PHONES

Shop around and switch plans or carriers. You can save big! In my family, we used to have one smart phone and two "dumb" phones with a giant cell phone carrier. We switched to a smaller, but still good carrier, and are saving a ton. Also, we have no contract tying us down. We now have three smart phones (not one) and pay one-third as much as we did with the old provider. We save about $200 a month, or $2,400 a year. Over ten years, we'll save a whopping $24,000! Many cell phone carriers today will even buy you out of your old contract.

Another cell phone tip is get your adult kids and other relatives off your plan. Why do you need to pay for your 30-year old's cell phone? Or if you want to keep a relative on your plan, tell them to start paying you $50 a month towards their share of the bill. That's only fair.

Finally, consider buying your phone instead of making monthly payments that add to your bill. You can get a barely used cellphone online for half the cost. Also, you may need a phone, but it doesn't have to be the most up-to-date iPhone! It is ridiculous to spend nearly $1,000 on a cell phone when its technology will be outdated in a year. Please, be smart about your smart phone!

<u>INSURANCE</u>

Many people stick with the same insurance carrier for life. If you never shop around, you don't know if you're paying too much. A number of years ago I decided that I would shop <u>all</u> our insurance that year. That included homeowner's insurance, car insurance, life insurance, umbrella insurance, and malpractice insurance. We switched multiple policies and saved a bundle.

We had been with a large car insurance company our whole adult lives. We started with this company because our parents used this company. When you have a male driver under 25 years old on your policy the premiums go up and up. We are members of AAA Roadside Assistance Club, so we used their free insurance brokerage service to shop for us. They found another national carrier, and our bill was slashed nearly in half.

Our homeowner's insurance was cut way down. Our umbrella policy was cut in half, and my malpractice insurance also decreased. All our insurance went down by simply spending the time to find better, less expensive policies.

You should also buy term life insurance instead of costly whole life insurance. You get more coverage for less money.

Finally, shop your health insurance as well, if you can. Maybe you've been on your spouse's health insurance plan for years. If so, be sure to check your own employer's plan to see if the terms aren't better the next year.

TRANSPORTATION

You may need a car to get to work, but you don't need the most expensive late model car out there. Don't buy a new car with high payments. Maybe you can afford it today, but what about tomorrow? I've seen people with car payments as high as other people's house payments. This is crazy! Also, never buy a brand-new car. Buy one that is one to three years old so you don't lose all the depreciation money. You see, when you buy a brand-new car and drive it off the lot, it immediately becomes a used car. Now it's worth less money than you owe for it. Ouch!

Consider skipping car payments all together. Save up a couple thousand dollars and buy a "junker" car that gets you from here to there. You can also carpool, share a car, or take the bus. When you're trying to get back on your feet, not having a car payment is a huge blessing and relief.

CABLE TV

Get rid of your cable, switch carriers, or just get basic cable and strip off all those premium channels. When our son was young, he played baseball on a team with many boys who came from lower income families. I once asked our son how he thought we measured up to the other families. He said, "Oh, we're a lot poorer than them. We don't have cable, a pool, or an X-Box." To this day, we are one of the few families in America who don't have cable, and that's fine by us. We have probably saved $75,000 over the last 32 years we've been married by skipping cable. That's a lot of money!

PAYDAY LOANS

Avoid these predatory loans at all costs! Payday loans are short term loans obtained by basically pledging your next pay check. The interest rates are astronomical (around 400% APR). It becomes a vicious cycle.

Typically, a person goes in to one of these big money lenders (or now just clicks a few buttons on the computer) and borrows, say $500. You are required to leave a post-dated check for $550. Then when you are paid the next week, you give them another post-dated check. Essentially you end up paying about $50 per week in interest on the initial $500 you borrowed. You'll never pay this off with such a high interest rate.

There is one big problem with payday loans: It is not illegal to owe money you can't repay, but it is illegal in many states to write a "bad" check, and that is what you have done by leaving them a post-dated check each week you go in.

Try to find another way to borrow the short-term emergency money you need until your next payday. Perhaps you can borrow something from a friend or family member. Is there a local charitable organization that will help you out for free? Some organizations will pay one month's electric bill or rent. Other organizations such as local churches and food banks will provide free groceries. Look around, and find another way before walking into one of these "Get cash now!" places.

OTHER DO'S AND DON'TS

Don't go to Starbucks and spend $5.00 on a cup of coffee. Brew your own at home. You could even invest $5.00 in a thermos and bring some with you if you're that desperate for a coffee fix on the way to work.

<u>Do</u> pay cash. <u>Don't</u> pay on credit cards. <u>Don't</u> go into debt. <u>Don't</u> play the lottery. It's a waste of money. And if you win, how much did it cost you to win that small prize? If you win big, i.e. "hit the lottery," odds are that you'll blow it in no time. People who have won the lottery have said it became a curse and not a blessing.

<u>Don't</u> ever co-sign a loan for your kid, friend, or anyone. And, Don't ask anyone to co-sign a loan for you. You will be putting each other's credit at risk and it's just not worth it.

<u>Don't</u> spend more than 25% of your net-take-home pay on rent or mortgage payments.

<u>Do</u> spend less than you make. <u>Don't</u> spend more than you make. I know this is common sense, but common sense isn't common, as they say.

The American way is to spend more as you earn more. Try keeping your living standard the same even as you make more money.

My husband and I bought our first and only home 30 years ago. We always said we'd keep it as long as the neighborhood stayed safe. We had the chance to trade up years ago, and I'm so very grateful that it didn't work out. You see, it was at the height of the housing boom that no one recognized was a bubble at the time. If we had bought the more expensive home, we would have been in a world of hurt the following year. Thank God that He doesn't always give us what we want, and He gives us what He wants us to have!

Speaking of houses, do <u>not</u> use your house as an ATM machine. I've seen so many people get in trouble when they take out a Home Equity Line of Credit (HELOC) or Home Equity Loan. This is a second mortgage on your house, and people don't even realize it. They put all their credit cards on the Line of Credit or make home improvements, etc. People may think they can deduct from their taxes the interest they pay on the HELOC, but with the 2018 tax law, that is no longer permitted. I recently heard a commercial that said, "Your house is your bank." Oh my goodness! Please, "Just say <u>No</u>!" like the old drug commercials. No, No, No – <u>Don't</u> take money out of your house for a vacation, a new car, or to pay off another loan. Don't do it!

<u>Do</u> build an emergency fund of $1,000. That way, if your car breaks down you have money to repair it, and you don't need to resort to credit cards.

<u>Do</u> sell stuff you don't need. Have a garage sale or sell things on e-bay. That can get you some money to start your emergency savings.

<u>Do</u> save three to six months of expenses as you are able so that you can survive a temporary interruption in your pay checks.

<u>Do</u> get on the same page with your spouse about finances. It's really important to communicate about money with

your spouse. Plan your budget together, decide how much you need to save for what goals, decide how much is a big decision that you two should discuss before one of you agrees to spend it.

<u>Do</u> learn to budget. (See Financial Education Section in Life Lessons for Bankruptcy Chapter.)

<u>Do</u> check your credit report six months after bankruptcy is done to make sure your Discharge shows on each of the three major credit bureau reports. All balances should be listed as zero dollars owed. And it should say something like "Included in Bankruptcy" without a ton of bad credit history. Go to www.annualcreditreport.com to get your credit reports for free.

<u>Do</u> keep your expenses down so you can survive in lean times. This is especially true if you are self-employed.

If you have other financial tips or Do's and Don'ts that have worked for you and you want to share with others, please contact me through my website,

www.bowenbankruptcylaw.com

I will be happy to include them in an updated book or blog.

Questions for Reflection

1. Do you think you need more income? Do you think you need to lower your expenses? Or, do you think you need a combination of the two?

_____

_____

_____

_____

_____

2. Are you a careful or thrifty shopper? If not, what changes can you make to spend less?

_____

_____

_____

_____

_____

_____

3. Are you paying bank service fees every month? If so, are you willing to investigate a cheaper alternative such as a local credit union?

_____

_____

_____

4. How can you save on your cell phone bills?

_____

_____

5. Are you willing to take the time to shop for insurance so you can get the best deal possible?

_____

6. What can you do to lower your transportation expenses?

_____

_____

_____

_____

_____

7. Are you willing to cut the cable TV cord?

_____

_____

8. Read through the Do's and Don'ts again. List each thing you plan to do or not do to secure a better financial future for yourself.

_____

_____

_____

_____

_____

_____

_____

_____

_____

_____

_____

_____

Beware of little expenses.
A small leak will sink
a great ship.

Benjamin Franklin

CHAPTER 10

At the End of the Day, It'll Be OK

MANY PEOPLE ARE REALLY HURTING right now. Perhaps you feel afraid, worried, conflicted, ashamed, embarrassed, exhausted, depressed, weak, hopeless, broken. These are all normal feelings when you are experiencing financial burdens beyond your control. But once you gather information, learn options, make a decision, and start taking action to resolve your financial problems, you'll start feeling much better. I've had clients tell me over the years that after bankruptcy they can breathe again, sleep better. It improved their heath. Saved their marriage. After bankruptcy, people have said, "It's the best decision I've ever made." I can't guarantee you anything. No lawyer can. But I can share with you these experiences of my clients over many years.

Often we don't know why we've had to go through hard times. "Is all my suffering and misery really necessary?" you may ask God. It could be that God is testing your faith, or that He wants to discipline you. Or it may be that you'll never know why you experienced financial troubles.

The Apostle Peter said:

For a little while you may have had to suffer grief in all kinds of trials. These have come so that the proven genuineness of your faith – of greater worth than gold, which perishes even though refined by fire – may result in praise, glory and honor when Jesus Christ is revealed.

1 Peter 1:6-7

Peter is emphasizing that faith is more precious than gold. You can lose all your money, but if you still have your faith through the trial, you have everything you need.

With faith, you'll know that "The Lord upholds all who fall and lifts up all who are bowed down." (Psalm 145:14).

Sometimes people are absolutely insistent on keeping some property, when it's not a good idea. When Mark and Linda fell behind in their mortgage payments and other bills, they decided to file a Chapter 13 bankruptcy to catch up on their payments. Their house was worth saving, as they had built up some equity over the years and the payment was relatively low and affordable at $1,100 per month.

The problem Mark and Linda had while in bankruptcy was that, although they both had good jobs and could pay the house payment, they also were carrying two rather large car payments that added up to more than their mortgage payment. They also had family who always seemed to need help and they had a hard time saying "No". They could not keep up with everything.

I told them they needed to ask themselves a question: "Which is more important to you, to keep your home, or to keep two expensive cars? Your house is an asset that should appreciate, or gain value over time. Your cars are assets which depreciate or lose value over time. Which makes more sense to keep when you can't keep it all?" The couple chose to let the most expensive car go back to the lender and they carpooled until a friend at work sold them his old car for $1,000. This was a huge blessing because the "new" car from their friend was quite reliable, and even though it had high mileage, it was worth much more than $1,000.

Mark and Linda were clutching their fists so tightly around their cars, that nothing good seemed to flow back to them. When they opened their hands and let the car go, their hands were now free to receive a new, unexpected blessing the Lord provided through the work friend.

Isaiah 49:8 reads,

This is what the LORD says: "In the time of my favor I will answer you, and in the day of salvation I will help you."

God may humble you now with hardship, but cry out to Him, and He'll save you from your distress. (See Psalm 107:12-13). Remember, God is good to the faithful in the end. (See Psalm 73).

A lot of times, people feel like they embody the modern-day Job. They may have one thing after another pile up on them where they are just drowning in debt and misfortune. Well, keep in mind that although God tested Job beyond any measure we can imagine, Job never lost his faith in God. Thus, at the end of the day, Job, who had lost his family, friends, all worldly possessions, and everything, was fully restored. (Job 42:10-17).

You may be depleted and defeated now, but "the Lord your God will restore your fortunes and have compassion on you." (Deuteronomy 30:3). Jesus, who healed the sick and raised the dead to life, can surely help restore you, not just financially, but spiritually, as well.

At the end of the day, it <u>will</u> be okay. You <u>will</u> get through this and things <u>will</u> get better.

In closing, I leave you with these beautiful words from the second letter of St. Paul to the Corinthians:

Finally, brothers and sisters, rejoice!
Strive for full restoration,
encourage one another,
be of one mind, live in peace.
And the God of love and peace
will be with you.

2 Corinthians 13:11

Questions for Reflection

1. Circle any of the following feelings you are experiencing or have experienced related to your financial situation:

Afraid
Worried
Conflicted
Ashamed
Embarrassed
Exhausted
Weak
Hopeless
Broken

2. Read Isaiah 49:8. Do you believe God might have something better in store for you later?

_____

_____

_____

_____

_____

_____

3. Write down your personal prayer to God right now. What's on your mind and in your heart? What are you thankful for? What do you need help with?

_____

_____

_____

_____

_____

_____

_____

4. What is the most important thing you have learned from this book? What is your personal take-away that you will act on now?

_____

_____

_____

_____

_____

_____

_____

Acknowledgements

First, I want to thank God for laying this book on my heart and giving me the courage to see it through. *"Entrust your works to the Lord and your plans will succeed."* *(Proverbs 16:3).* This has been the Word I've clung to throughout this project.

The fact that you are holding a book in your hands now is a testament to the goodness of the Lord. If I help but one person, my plans have succeeded. Hopefully, many more will be helped, but that is up to God.

Next, I want to thank my constant companion and partner on this journey called life, my love, inspiration, my college sweetheart, my husband of 32 years, Hugh. Thank you for your unwavering love, your faithfulness, and your attention to every word I wrote. I am so grateful for your patience and your valuable insight and comments on each chapter of the book. Thank you for supporting my passion to help people with financial problems find a better way.

Thank you to my son Alex, my pride and joy. I look forward to the day when we will soon be fellow lawyers. And to your sweet fiancée Taylor, thank you for loving and supporting my son as much as I love his father. I look forward to you officially joining the family.

For my parents, Bill and Marie Lindsey, married 67 years until Mom's passing, thank you for a firm foundation in faith. Thank you also to my dad for teaching me early in life about financial responsibility. It is upon these building blocks that I am able to help people in financial distress find peace every day.

Thank you to the following church/spiritual leaders who offered valuable guidance and suggestions on this project: Rev. Ralph DuWell, Rev. Joseph O'Neil, Pastor Melanie Ruta (thank you for checking every Bible quote!), Pastor Ed DeWitt, Minister Henry Bady, and especially Pastor Tim Grosshans and Rev. N. S. Augustine Clark who gave so generously of their time, wisdom, and Biblical, theological, historical, and practical knowledge. Thank you all for making sure I did not lead anyone down the wrong path!

Thank you to the Hon. Karen S. Jennemann, U.S. Bankruptcy Judge, who shared her historical knowledge of debtor's prisons and verified bankruptcy principles in conjunction with the Bible.

Thank you to my friends and colleagues Rebecca Forest, Robert Hoofman, Laurie Weatherford, Lori Patton, and

Emerson Noble. Thank you to Danielle Merola, Josh Grosshans, and Joan Peterson for opening doors.

Thanks to Ruth Stern and Joe Bilello for breakthrough help with the sub-title. Thank you to John Zoll for the idea to include a section on examination of financial conscience. Thanks to Marilyn Young for library help. Thanks to Nanette Schimpf for marketing help and encouragement.

Thank you to my Dave Ramsey Entreleadership Mastermind Group who held me accountable along the way: Coach Brian Lawrence, Jordan Baker, Jeff Watson, Esq., Sam Taggert, Eric and Marie Olson, Millard Ledford, Kristi Horton, and Robert Schnell.

Special thanks to Ed Alexander and Charlie Price, fellow lawyers, authors, and friends for great ideas and enormous amounts of encouragement.

I am very grateful to my wonderful office team, Christie Smith for incredible typing and comments, to Tara Glasco who kept the office running smoothly all along, and to Suzanne Alamina who joined Team Bowen in time to enthusiastically embrace this ministry.

To my amazing book cover designer and typesetter, Donna Cunningham of Beaux Arts Design, who perfectly captured the essence of the book with her beautiful cover design.

To my dedicated editor, who just happens to be my sister, Carol A. Barnett, who painstakingly read and re-read every word, sentence and thought. Thank you for all your support, encouragement, pride, and love.

Finally, thank you to my clients, past, present, and future - - many who have encouraged me in this project and have gladly shared their stories with me. Thank you all for entrusting me with your financial and legal matters and allowing me to guide you to financial freedom and peace.

Blessings,

Anne-Marie L. Bowen

About the Author

ANNE-MARIE L. BOWEN IS A Christian Florida attorney called to minister to financially weary souls. She has been practicing bankruptcy law for more than 20 years in Orlando, Florida. She has helped thousands of people resolve their financial problems through legal counseling, negotiating with creditors, and filing bankruptcy.

Attorney Bowen is the past President of the Central Florida Bankruptcy Law Association and is also the past Chairman of the Bankruptcy Committee of the Orange County Bar Association. She is a member of the American Bankruptcy Institute, the National Association of Chapter Thirteen Trustees, and the National Association of Consumer Bankruptcy Attorneys.

Anne-Marie Bowen is also the author of the book for consumers, <u>Bankruptcy... Because Life Happens.</u> She proudly helps people in financial distress find peace.

To contact the author or order additional books, go to <u>www.bowenbankruptcylaw.com</u> , or call 407-228-1300.